# Voices for Green Choices

# Al Gore

## A Wake-Up Call to Global Warming

*By Dale Anderson*

# Crabtree Publishing Company

www.crabtreebooks.com

# Crabtree Publishing Company

**Author:** Dale Anderson
**Publishing plan research and development:**
  Sean Charlebois, Reagan Miller
  Crabtree Publishing Company
**Editor:** Lynn Peppas
**Proofreader:** Crystal Sikkens
**Project coordinator:** Robert Walker
**Content and curriculum adviser:** Suzy Gazlay, M.A.
**Editorial:** Mark Sachner
**Photo research:** Ruth Owen
**Design:** Westgraphix/Tammy West
**Production coordinator:** Margaret Amy Salter
**Prepress technicians:** Margaret Amy Salter, Ken Wright

Written, developed, and produced by Water Buffalo Books

Cover photo: A dramatic photo of a glacier calving, or breaking off a huge chunk of ice. Between 1995 and 2002 alone, half a dozen ice sheets larger than the state of Rhode Island broke off Antarctica because of rising temperatures there.

**Photo credits:**
Corbis: Daniel A. Anderson/Orange County Register:
  page 5 (bottom); Bjorn Sigurdson: page 8 (bottom);
  Bettmann: page 9 (left); Bettmann: page 12 (bottom);
  Sygma: page 13 (bottom); Bettmann: page 14 (left);
  Bettmann: page 17 (bottom); Bettmann:
  page 18 (bottom); Jeffrey Markowitz/Sygma:
  page 21 (bottom); Bettmann: page 23 (top);
  Bettman: page 25 (bottom); Peter Turnley:
  page 28 (left); Peter Turnley: page 29 (bottom);
  Orban Thierry: page 32 (top); Roger Ressmeyer:
  page 33 (bottom)
FLPA: Reinhard Dirscherl: page 15 (bottom);
  Reinhard Dirscherl: page 34 (center)
Getty Images: page 24 (top); Dean Mouhtaropoulos:
  page 4 (left); Ed Clark: page 10 (bottom);
  Consolidated News Pictures: page 18 (top);
  Mike Nelson: page 19 (right); Robert King:
  page 35 (right); J. Emilio Flores: page 37 (top)
International Rivers: Glenn Switkes: page 27 (top)
NASA: page 38 (center and bottom)
Shutterstock: front cover, pages 1, 7, 11 (right),
  16 (bottom), 20 (left), 22 (top), 26 (bottom),
  27 (bottom), 30 (top), 31 (bottom), 34 (left),
  36 (left), 38 (top), 39 (bottom), 40, 41, 42
Wikimedia Commons: public domain image

**Library and Archives Canada Cataloguing in Publication**

Anderson, Dale, 1953-
    Al Gore : a wake-up call to global warming / Dale Anderson.

(Voices for green choices)
Includes index.
ISBN 978-0-7787-4666-9 (bound).--ISBN 978-0-7787-4679-9 (pbk.)

    1. Gore, Albert, 1948- --Juvenile literature. 2. United States.
Congress. Senate--Biography--Juvenile literature. 3. Environmental-
ists--United States--Biography--Juvenile literature. 4. Nobel Prize
winners--United States--Biography--Juvenile literature. 5. Global
warming-- Juvenile literature. 6. Vice-Presidents--United States--
Biography-- Juvenile literature. I. Title. II. Series: Voices for
green choices

E840.8.G65A54 2009          j363.738'74          C2009-900028-8

**Library of Congress Cataloging-in-Publication Data**

Anderson, Dale, 1953-
  Al Gore : a wake-up call to global warming / by Dale Anderson.
    p. cm. -- (Voices for green choices)
  Includes index.
  ISBN 978-0-7787-4679-9 (pbk. : alk. paper)
  --ISBN 978-0-7787-4666-9 (reinforced lib. bdg. : alk. paper)
  1. Gore, Albert, 1948---Juvenile literature. 2. Environmentalists--
United States--Biography--Juvenile literature. 3. Nobel Prize win-
ners--United States--Biography--Juvenile literature. 4. Global
warming--Juvenile literature. 5. United States. Congress. Senate--
Biography--Juvenile literature. 6. Vice-Presidents--United States--
Biography--Juvenile literature. 7. Vice-Presidential candidates--
United States--Biography--Juvenile literature. I. Title. II. Series.

  GE56.G67A53 2009
  363.738'74--dc22
                                                    2008054508

# Crabtree Publishing Company

www.crabtreebooks.com          1-800-387-7650

**Published in Canada**
**Crabtree Publishing**
616 Welland Ave.
St. Catharines, Ontario
L2M 5V6

**Published in the United States**
**Crabtree Publishing**
PMB16A
350 Fifth Ave., Suite 3308
New York, NY 10118

**Published in the United Kingdom**
**Crabtree Publishing**
White Cross Mills
High Town, Lancaster
LA1 4XS

**Published in Australia**
**Crabtree Publishing**
386 Mt. Alexander Rd.
Ascot Vale (Melbourne)
VIC 3032

# Contents

## Chapter 1

# Winning the Prize

On October 12, 2007, the Norwegian Nobel Committee announced the winner of that year's Nobel Peace Prize. The Peace Prize is given annually to a person or group that has done "the most or the best work for fraternity between nations, for the abolition or reduction of standing armies and for the holding of peace congresses." In some years, the committee giving this prize has moved beyond this definition to recognize people who promote human rights or improve the lives of masses living in poverty.

The year 2007 marked one of those departures. That year, the Nobel Peace Prize was awarded to Albert Gore, Jr. of the United States and to a United Nations panel of scientists, the Intergovernmental Panel on Climate Change. Al Gore and the group of scientists were recognized, the committee said, "for their efforts to build up and disseminate greater knowledge about man-made climate change."

## An Inconvenient Truth

Al Gore first became concerned about climate change as a college student. Later, when he served in the United States Congress, he led committee hearings investigating evidence that the world's climate was changing and looking into the effects of that change.

▲ Al Gore issues a stark warning in *An Inconvenient Truth:* "Not only does human-caused global warming exist, but it is also growing more and more dangerous, and at a pace that has now made it a planetary emergency."

He also introduced some laws aimed at slowing down the rate of global warming.

Al's main work in the field came after he lost his bid to be elected president of the United States in 2000. After that defeat, he dedicated himself to raising awareness about the causes and consequences of global warming. Traveling the world, he talked to audiences while presenting a slide show with charts, graphs, and photographs that dramatized the growing threat of global warming.

Movie producers had the idea of turning that show into a film and hired director Davis Guggenheim to direct it. In 2006, Guggenheim released his documentary, called *An Inconvenient Truth*. Much of the movie is simply Al delivering his slide show. Vivid footage of weather disasters and the collapse of vast sheets of ice at the North and South Poles underscores the message.

A few months after Al received the Nobel Prize, *An Inconvenient Truth* earned another honor, the Academy Award for best documentary film of the year. In the movie, and in a book with the same title,

*"We, the human species, are confronting a planetary emergency—a threat to the survival of our civilization that is gathering ominous and destructive potential even as we gather here. But there is hopeful news as well: we have the ability to solve this crisis and avoid the worst—though not all—of its consequences, if we act boldly, decisively and quickly."*

- Al Gore speaking on accepting his Nobel Prize in 2007

◄ In February 2008, Al Gore (left) and film director Davis Guggenheim posed with the Oscar won by *An Inconvenient Truth*. The Academy Award was a tribute to the impact Al had with his message about global warming.

## Nobel Prizes

The Nobel Prizes are among the world's most prominent awards. The prizes were created at the direction of Alfred Nobel, a Swedish scientist and business leader who built a fortune making dynamite. When Nobel died in 1896, he left his huge fortune to fund prizes to be awarded each year in five fields that interested him—physics, chemistry, physiology or medicine, literature, and promoting peace. A sixth prize, in economics, was added in 1969.

Winners of the prize receive more than one million dollars. While that sum is substantial, it is not the money that appeals to prize winners. Rather, it is the honor of being named worthy of one of the world's most prestigious awards.

Al laid out four key points:

- The overall average temperature of Earth's atmosphere has been rising rapidly in recent decades.
- Human activity—mainly the burning of fossil fuels, which produce greenhouse gases—is the chief cause of that temperature rise.
- If temperatures continue to go up, humans will see a host of natural disasters, including droughts that will ruin crops, severe storms that will damage property and kill people, and sea levels that will rise to flood low-lying coastal areas and islands.
- People can prevent these disasters, but they must start taking steps to do so immediately.

## The Co-Winner

Al's co-winner was the Intergovernmental Panel on Climate Change (IPCC), formed by the United Nations in 1988. More than 2,000 scientists take part in this group. Its purpose is to review scientific research on climate change and make recommendations to governments about how real the threat is.

## Speaking Out on Global Warming

Rajendra Pachauri, of India, the head of the IPCC, accepted the prize on behalf of that group. In his Nobel lecture, Pachauri spoke of the important role

◄ Alfred Nobel may have been inspired to endow a peace prize by a close friend, Bertha von Suttner, who was active in the peace movement and who won the prize in 1905.

young people can play in solving the problem. He said that young people around the world should put pressure on adults to make needed changes and to keep the world livable.

Al urged the nations of the world to take several specific actions to slow the growth of greenhouse gas emissions, which cause global warming. He singled out the United States and China for criticism because those two nations

## Global Warming Facts

In *An Inconvenient Truth*, Al Gore lists several troubling facts about global warming:

• $CO_2$, or carbon dioxide, is a gas found naturally in the atmosphere. Burning fossil fuels releases $CO_2$ into the atmosphere. In the past 650,000 years, levels of $CO_2$ in the air never surpassed 300 parts per million. In 2005, some locations on Earth posted levels nearing 400 parts per million.

• Scientists studying Earth's overall average temperature from 1860 to 2005 found that 20 of the 21 hottest years occurred between 1980 and 2005.

• The vast sheets of ice in the Arctic Circle and in Antarctica help cool Earth. The amount of ice covering the Arctic has fallen from more than 5.2 million square miles (13.5 million sq km) in 1900 to less than 4.6 million square miles (12 million sq km) in 2005.

▶ Al Gore and the IPCC say that burning fossil fuels— coal, oil, and natural gas— causes global warming.

◀ Between 1995 and 2002 alone, half a dozen ice sheets larger than the state of Rhode Island broke off Antarctica because of rising temperatures there.

burn the most fossil fuels but, up to that point, had not agreed to taking specific actions to cut emissions. He warned that taking steps would be painful and would involve costs, but that the cost of not acting was worse.

In awarding the joint prize, the Nobel Committee purposefully honored two distinct achievements. It gave the IPCC the award to honor its disciplined scientific study of the issue. Al won his share of the prize, the committee said, because he was "probably the single individual who has done most to create greater worldwide understanding of the measures that need to be adopted" to reverse climate change.

▲ Al Gore and Rajendra Pachauri proudly display the diplomas and gold medals they received in recognition of the 2007 Nobel Peace Prize. Pachauri accepted on behalf of the Intergovernmental Panel on Climate Change (IPCC).

## Chapter 2

▲ Albert Gore, Sr. (left) helps son Albert, Jr. hold a bow and arrow the boy had just received. Al's parents taught their son about life, family, the land, and politics.

Albert Gore, Jr. was raised by loving but demanding parents and grew up in two places that both shaped him. In Washington, D.C., where he lived most of the year, his family was deeply involved in politics. At his family's home in Tennessee, in the summers, he learned to feel close to the land.

### Albert and Pauline Gore

Al's father, Albert Gore, Sr., came from a poor family in a poor town in central Tennessee. He was determined, though, to escape poverty. He became the first person in his town to ever go to college when he enrolled in a state teacher's college in Tennessee. While studying, he took odd jobs to earn enough money to live on.

Eventually, Albert, Sr. began to teach and soon after was named the principal of a school. Within a few years, he decided to study law. After working at school during the day, he took night classes at the Vanderbilt University Law School. While at Vanderbilt, Albert, Sr., met Pauline LaFon. Born in western Tennessee, she too was attending law school—and waiting on tables in a coffee shop to pay her bills.

Albert and Pauline fell in love and were married in 1937. The two newlyweds were

## House and Senate

Congress is the branch of the United States government that makes the laws. It is divided into two chambers, the Senate and the House of Representatives. The Senate has two members from each state. The number of members a state has in the House depends on its population. The more people living in a state, the more representatives the state has. Each House member represents a part of the state called a district. Senators serve six-year terms. Members of the House stand for re-election every two years. Since they have to answer to their constituents more often, they have to be more responsive to them. Members of Congress can show this responsiveness in three ways:

- By writing and voting for laws that will help constituents
- By convincing Congress to spend federal dollars on projects that will help the district or state
- By helping constituents solve problems with government agencies

not only deeply in love, they also had complementary talents. Albert, Sr. was a thinker and man of principle. Pauline Gore was a savvy politician. Her husband had decided on a career in politics, and her skills would help him greatly.

Albert Gore, Sr.'s first office was as a state labor commissioner. He began serving in that office the year before the couple married. In 1938, the couple's first child was born, Nancy LaFon Gore. That same year, Albert ran for Congress, and won. He managed to win re-election several times, serving in the House continuously until 1953 except for a brief period when he was in the army.

On March 31, 1948, Albert, Sr. and Pauline had a second child, a boy whom they named Albert Gore, Jr.

▲ The Gores (from left: Pauline, Al, Albert, Sr., and Nancy) enjoy some family time at home. Al's sister Nancy had a genuine fondness for her "baby" brother and called him "Bo."

## Growing Up in Washington

During his childhood, young Al spent most of the year in Washington, D.C., a bustling city devoted to politics, where his father served in Congress. He spent his summers at the family farm back in Tennessee. Here, he saw a natural world of trees, creeks, fields, and rocks. Years later, in *An Inconvenient Truth*, Al would remember the lessons he learned about the land from his father during his summers on the farm. Those lessons shaped Al's deep concern for the environment.

Summers back on the farm were not all fun. They were also marked by hard work. Al's chores would begin at dawn, when he rose from his bed to tend to the family's cattle and hogs. During the hot afternoon, he had to labor in the fields. This regime was partly a political calculation on the part of Albert, Sr. Thinking that young Al might one day run for political office in Tennessee, his father wanted to make sure his son could prove he had lived in, and understood, the state. Albert, Sr. had another important goal in mind, too. He wanted his son to learn self-discipline and respect for hard work.

Albert, Sr. was demanding. He was also always teaching. When Al asked Albert, Sr. a question, his father often responded with long lectures.

*"As a kid, I often walked with my father over every part of the place, learning from him to appreciate the details of the terrain. My dad taught me the moral necessity of caring for the land. He never used those exact words, but that's what his lessons were all about."*

- Al Gore writing about his boyhood summers on the family farm in Tennessee, from *An Inconvenient Truth*

▶ As a child, Al hiked along streams like this one and fished and canoed in calmer water. In adulthood, he and his wife and children often went on camping trips to be close to nature.

## Taking a Stand

The Gore family chose to send young Al to St. Albans School for several reasons. First, it had a strong religious and moral backbone. This appealed to the Gores' sense of discipline and responsibility. Second, it gave students a strong academic grounding. Finally, there was another reason, one that strongly reflected the Gore family's values. St. Albans had African American students. This was unusual for private schools in Washington at that time. This factor appealed to Pauline Gore's sense of the equality of the races.

The lessons his father taught stuck. At a camp in Tennessee when Al was 12, other boys mocked him for being a soft city boy. Al's response was not to fight or to sulk. Instead, he volunteered to work in the kitchen, a task usually set aside for older campers. By taking on that difficult work, he hoped to impress the other campers that he was not a privileged son.

## Growing Up in Washington

After many years in the House, Albert, Sr. was first elected to the Senate in 1952. Re-elected twice, he remained there until 1971. In the Senate, he was highly independent. He did not vote in favor of his own party's bills if he did not feel they were right. He voted for various civil rights laws, taking a stance that would not help him win re-election in Tennessee. At the time, many white voters in Tennessee opposed these laws. When Lyndon B. Johnson was president, United States involvement in the Vietnam War grew rapidly. Senator Gore, like Johnson, was a Democrat, but Gore spoke out often against the war.

In fourth grade, Al began to attend St. Albans School, one of the top private high schools in Washington, D.C. Teachers at St. Albans liked Al because he worked hard and was disciplined. He was a good student, but not an excellent one.

▼ Albert Gore, Sr. (center) celebrates an election win in 1958 along with Pauline and young Al. Al's father was a man of principle whom his son later called "the greatest man I ever knew in my life."

When he graduated, he was in the middle of his class—25th out of 51 students.

Al was very competitive, and at least once got into a fight with a classmate who challenged him. He played offensive line in football, a position without glamour. In basketball, he was known for his jump shot.

Students who edited Al's high school yearbook predicted he would gain success some day, adding that when it happened, none of his classmates would be surprised.

## A Special Meeting

Shortly before Al graduated from high school, he went to a dance with a girl he had been dating in Tennessee. There he met Mary Elizabeth Aitcheson. The attractive, lively Mary Elizabeth was nicknamed "Tipper." Al and Tipper were instantly attracted to each other. They stayed with their own dates that night, but Al called Tipper the next day and asked her to another party. As Tipper later recalled, "We put on a record and danced and danced. It was like everyone else melted away. We've been together ever since."

### A Strong Moral Code

While at St. Albans, Al adopted, and lived by, the school's strong moral code. The code required that students do the right thing, even if it was difficult, rather than the wrong thing, even if it was easy.

One year, a math teacher mistakenly handed out an exam from the prior year. Since it was a repeat exam, Al and another student knew all the answers. Rather than take the test, they told the teacher. Al also demonstrated his strong moral compass in other ways. In his junior year, he befriended a student who was a newcomer to the school and friendless. On another occasion, when a couple of bullying students teased another boy who was not part of the "in group," Al shamed them into stopping.

► Al Gore and Tipper Aitcheson (right) began dating after they met at a dance. In his dedication in *An Inconvenient Truth*, Al calls Tipper "my beloved wife and partner. . .who has been with me for the entire journey."

## Chapter 3

# College, Army, and After

▲ While Al was at Harvard, students opposed to the Vietnam War seized one of the college administration buildings. Police moved in to clear the occupants out, striking some with nightsticks, an action that angered many other students.

A l Gore graduated from St. Albans in 1965. The next nine years would shape his thinking and his politics. During this period, Al first learned about the potential problem of global warming, began his family, and searched for a career.

## Al at Harvard

In the fall of 1965, Al arrived at Harvard College in Cambridge, Massachusetts. Early in his first year, he allowed his political ambitions to be known. While sitting around with other students talking about their goals, Al flatly stated that he wanted to be president one day. A fellow student later recalled that the others all laughed at such plain and lofty ambition.

To put his ambitions to work, Al ran for class council and won. The experience was not a happy one. His closest friends ridiculed campus politics as trivial, and after serving out the year, Al never ran for school office again.

Another formative experience was a seminar Al attended during his first year. The instructor was Martin Peretz, at the time a radical leftist. (Years later, Peretz became the publisher and editor of *The New Republic* magazine and took more moderate positions on some issues.) The seminar had only a dozen students, each picked by Peretz. He led his students to think critically about how society was organized and to challenge their assumptions about right and wrong. Some of the students adopted more radical views as a result of the readings and discussions. Al did not, but he did learn to question, rather than accept, how society worked.

Al was at the center of a diverse group of friends that included Tommy Lee Jones, the future movie star and leader of the group. Starting in his second year, Al also spent a lot of time with Tipper Aitcheson, who came to Boston for college after graduating from high school.

Two classes that Al took in his third year influenced him deeply. One was a science class taught by Professor Roger Revelle. Since the late 1950s, Revelle had been measuring levels of $CO_2$ in Hawaii and watching them rise. He was concerned that the buildup of $CO_2$ could change the world's climate if it continued. Years later, Al would

*"It was obvious to our small group that he (Professor Roger Revelle) himself was surprised and disturbed by how quickly the $CO_2$ was building up (in Hawaii). And more important, he understood—and communicated forcefully to us—what the likely implications of this data would turn out to be. He knew that this path our civilization had taken would send us careening toward catastrophe, unless the trend could be reversed."*

- Al Gore talks about the ideas of his Harvard science teacher, Professor Roger Revelle, in *An Inconvenient Truth*

◄ One worrying implication of global warming is the melting of polar ice caps, which will cause sea levels to rise. The rising ocean waters could then flood low-lying areas, such as this beach in Hawaii, where this turtle lays its eggs.

## A Divisive War

The United States began fighting in Vietnam in the early 1960s. It supported the government of South Vietnam, which was fighting against communist rebels called the Viet Cong and troops sent by the communist government of North Vietnam. At first, only a few hundred American troops served in Vietnam, and their role was limited to that of advisors. Starting in 1965, though, the number of troops rose sharply and rapidly, and American soldiers played a larger role in combat. Casualties began to mount.

Most of these troops were young men who had been drafted. The war, and the draft, became the focus of a bitter national debate. "Doves" wanted to end both the war and the draft, charging that the war was immoral and the draft unfair. "Hawks" said the war was needed to stop the spread of communism. Opposition to the war forced President Lyndon Johnson to decide not to seek re-election in 1968. After becoming president by winning the 1968 election, Richard Nixon ended the draft and began pulling American troops out of Vietnam.

explain, in *An Inconvenient Truth,* the impact that Revelle's ideas had had on him. Revelle's science class planted the seed of Al's later environmental work.

The other influential class was government professor Richard Neustadt's course on the American presidency. Fascinated by the course, Al changed majors from English to government.

## Key Decisions

When Al graduated from Harvard in 1969, he faced a difficult decision. Once he graduated from college, he was subject to the draft. If drafted, he was likely to be sent to Vietnam. While Al had not taken part in campus protests against the war in Vietnam, he did oppose the war. Not going into the army, on the other hand, would endanger his father's chance of winning re-election. The senator would seem unpatriotic if his son did not serve. Senator Gore had struggled to win re-election in 1964 and was likely to face a serious challenge in 1970.

▶ More than 58,200 names of Americans who died, or are still missing in action, are engraved on the Vietnam Veterans Memorial in Washington, D.C. The memorial was dedicated in 1982, after the bitter war had ended.

Al wrestled with the decision for several weeks. In the end, he decided to enlist. As an enlistee, he had a better chance of being assigned to a non-combat role and perhaps avoid Vietnam. Nevertheless, the 21-year-old's decision put duty to his father, and his country, ahead of his own desires.

After basic training Al was given a non-combat assignment as an army journalist. He was sent to Fort Rucker, in Alabama. A few months later, Al took another major step. He and Tipper married on May 19, 1970, in Washington, D.C. The Gores began married life living on a private's small pay in a trailer near Al's base.

Some weekends, Al was granted leave. He traveled up to Tennessee to campaign for his father's re-election. Al appeared in uniform, hoping that the sight might weaken voters' anger about Senator Gore's anti-war position. The senator's Republican opponent pushed hard at issues that hurt him with voters, however, and Gore lost. Al took two lessons from his father's defeat. He believed that his father lost because the people saw him as too liberal for them, and had not done a good enough job taking care of constituents.

▼ These young men were sworn into the army after being drafted. Al was also sworn in, although he volunteered to serve.

## Private Gore

In the midst of his father's campaign, Al received orders for Vietnam. He arrived in Vietnam in January of 1971. At that point in the war, President Richard Nixon was reducing the number of American troops and forcing South Vietnam to take on more of the fighting. Morale was low among troops. Drug use was high.

Al was assigned as the public relations officer for an engineering unit. His job was to write stories for the unit's newspaper and magazine and to send to local papers back in the United States. Al never saw any combat action and was never in any real danger. Workdays were full of routine tasks. Evenings were spent with other army reporters telling jokes or playing basketball. Just three months into his tour in Vietnam, orders came for his engineering unit to return to the States. Al returned to the United States in May 1971.

## Back Home

Back in Tennessee, Al began taking classes at Vanderbilt University's Divinity School. He had no interest in training for the ministry, but he did feel the need to study spiritual and ethical matters. One of these courses might have influenced his later thinking. The course emphasized the idea of humankind's responsibility to care for Earth.

▲ Albert Gore, Sr., shown in the Senate in 1969, opposed the war in Vietnam and never asked his son to enlist. But Al knew that doing so would help his father's political career.

▼ When Al arrived in Vietnam, United States combat troops still faced the tension of knowing that they were in constant danger.

While attending school, Al worked at night at the *Nashville Tennessean*, a prominent, and generally liberal, newspaper. Since he was new, Al was given low-level assignments, such as the police beat and special events such as "Hillbilly Day." After a year at the Divinity School, Al left to work on the *Tennessean* full time. After taking a special course on investigative reporting in 1972, Al began covering more political stories and became more interested in political issues. In August of 1974, he took a leave of absence from the paper to begin attending Vanderbilt's law school. The decision to attend law school pleased his parents. They saw this as the first step toward a political career.

By this time, Al and Tipper had their first child, a daughter they named Karenna. When Karenna was two, Tipper began working at the *Tennessean* as an assistant in the photography lab and later as a photographer.

In the summer of 1975, Al returned part-time to the *Tennessean* and joined the editorial board—the group of top editors who meet to decide the paper's position on various issues and then write editorials expressing that view. Al continued that work when he resumed law classes later in the year.

▲ Tipper's work as a photographer at the *Tennessean* became the basis of a lifelong interest in photography. Some of her photos appear in her husband's books, including *An Inconvenient Truth*.

## Chapter 4

▲ The United States Capitol is home to both the House of Representatives and the Senate. In 1977, it became the base of Al Gore's political career.

**B**eginning in 1977, Al Gore spent his next 16 years in Congress, serving first in the House of Representatives and then in the Senate. Over time he became a prominent national political leader. He was known as a hard worker who deeply cared about issues—especially the environment.

### Winning His First Election

Early in 1976, Al learned that the member of the United States House from Tennessee's fourth district—Albert Gore, Sr.'s, old seat—was going to retire. Al quickly made a decision that he would try to win the seat. He left law school to campaign full time. Al first had to win the Democratic primary. Remembering his father's 1970 defeat, he tried to avoid seeming too liberal. To look more acceptable and more serious, he cut his long hair and began wearing sober blue suits. He also took some positions that ran counter to those he had expressed in editorials. For instance, he said that he did not want stricter laws controlling people's access to guns.

Al campaigned from dawn to dusk, visiting some towns four or five times. The night of the primary, August 5, Al won with 32 percent of the vote in a field of nine.

Since the Republicans ran no candidate for the seat that November, Al was assured of being elected.

## A Complex Record

Early in January of 1977, Al was sworn in as a member of Congress. He quickly threw himself into the work. He joined other new members in urging House leaders to televize floor debates, which had never been done before. The House finally adopted that rule in 1979, and on March 19 of that year the cameras were turned on for the first time. The first member to speak was Al Gore.

Al worked hard for his constituents. He set up offices throughout the district to handle complaints or problems that people had. He returned home regularly to listen to voters' concerns.

Politically, Al took positions in the middle ground, calling himself a "raging moderate." He was willing to have the government

*"My family and I know the bitterness of defeat. I have a family that teaches you what public service is all about. That is what my family has taught me. I consider the office of congressman a sacred trust."*

- Following his election to Congress in 1976, Al Gore remembers his father's 1970 defeat in his victory speech

▼   Al, shown campaigning for Congress in 1976, chats with a group of farmers in Tennessee. Al never forgot the importance of understanding the people of the state he represented in Washington.

▶ In the 1970s, the cigarette industry came under increasingly harsh criticism because of the harmful health effects of smoking. The growing unpopularity of tobacco posed a problem for tobacco farmers in Tennessee.

become involved in solving some problems, like a liberal, but he also favored other programs that liberals opposed. He backed a law to put sharp warning labels on cigarette packages. At the same time, he supported the government's payment of price supports to tobacco farmers. He supported the nuclear freeze movement, where the liberals' goal was to build no more nuclear weapons, but voted to build the MX missile, which was a new weapons system. He chaired some hearings on environmental issues such as global warming, but he also voted for water projects in Tennessee that environmentalists did not like.

Al held some important hearings. One set looked at the environmental disaster found in a New York development called Love Canal. Homes there had been built near an underground storage area for poisonous chemicals. When those chemicals slowly leaked onto people's property, plants began dying and people developed illnesses. Al's hearing, and his work on the issue, led to the passage of the first Superfund bill.

◄ An abandoned home in Love Canal tells the sorry tale of the fate of this development. The dangers posed by toxic chemicals forced residents to leave.

The government uses money from the Superfund to clean up the nation's most environmentally dangerous sites.

In 1980, Al decided to become involved in the issue of the nuclear arms race between the United States and the Soviet Union. Al was genuinely concerned about the danger of nuclear war, but he was also looking for a high-profile issue so he could make a name for himself.

After two years of study on the issue, he introduced a plan in 1982 to reduce the number of warheads—individual nuclear bombs—each country placed on its missiles. Al's plan was never adopted, but he had established himself as a top thinker on national security issues.

## Family Happiness and Family Tragedy

Al won re-election in 1978, 1980, and 1982. During these years, he and Tipper had three more children: daughter Kristin in June 1977, daughter Sarah in January 1979, and son Albert III in October 1982.

▶ Al Gore's 1984 Senate victory—which he celebrates in this photo—signaled his popularity in Tennessee. While 59 percent of the state's voters chose Republican presidential candidate Ronald Reagan, Al, a Democrat, won 61 percent of the Senate votes.

Then, in 1982, tragedy hit. Al's beloved sister Nancy was diagnosed with lung cancer, probably caused by years of heavy smoking. Over the next two years she became increasingly ill, and died on July 11, 1984. Nancy's illness spurred Al to join the push for stronger warning labels on cigarette packages. He was the first member of Congress from a state that produced tobacco who worked aggressively for such a law.

## In the Senate

Meanwhile, one of Tennessee's two United States senators decided not to run for re-election in 1984. Al announced his candidacy for the seat in May. He ran a strong campaign against a weak opponent, and won by a wide margin.

When Al was sworn in as senator, his father told a family friend, "This is the beginning." The son apparently shared his father's ambition. Two years later, Al launched a campaign to become the Democratic nominee for president. The field was crowded, with eight candidates running. In the end, Al struggled to raise enough money and to differentiate himself. He did win six primaries in early March, but the showing was less than he had hoped for, and other candidates were getting bigger wins. After finishing poorly in other primaries and only winning ten percent of the vote in New York, Al dropped out of the race.

## A New Direction

Embarrassed by his poor showing, Al entered a period of soul searching. He found new energy by thinking about what he wanted to accomplish as a public official. One area he cared about was technology. In May of 1989, he introduced a bill in the Senate to connect government, universities, and businesses to the still small grouping of computer networks called the Internet. The bill, which passed in 1991, was instrumental in promoting the growth of the Internet.

### A Momentous Decision

Several factors entered into Al Gore's decision to run in the 1988 presidential election. In political terms, at the age of 39 Al was a young man. Al and his father believed that the country would be looking for a younger man to become president in 1988. With expertise in both domestic and national security issues, Al felt he had a better mix of experience than other candidates. Finally, Al thought he would benefit from the sequence of the Democratic primaries. Early in the process, Democrats in 20 states in the South and West would hold primaries. Those voters, Al thought, would find a moderate like him appealing.

◄ In April 1988, Al Gore announced that he was suspending his campaign for the Democratic nomination for president. For the first time, Al faced defeat in his pursuit of a political office.

## Earth in the Balance

Al Gore's book, *Earth in the Balance*, was a deeply felt, closely reasoned argument for dramatic changes in how people live. Al explored the connections he saw between human thinking and institutions and global warming and pollution. He outlined an ambitious plan to solve the environmental crisis. Steps included slowing worldwide population growth, helping poorer countries build their economies without harming the environment, and cutting greenhouse gas emissions.

Environmentalists compared Al's book to Rachel Carson's famous 1962 book *Silent Spring*. Critics said that Al exaggerated the seriousness of the problem and ignored the potential costs of his solutions.

The other issue that Al became increasingly involved in was the environment. He started thinking about writing a book about the dangers of pollution and the problem of global warming—the issue raised by Professor Revelle's class back at Harvard.

## Spreading the Word

Early in 1989, a new tragedy struck the Gore family. Young Albert, who was only six, was hit by a car and nearly died. The accident convinced Al and Tipper to spend less time on their careers, and more time with their children. Al decided not to run for president again in 1992. As he explained, "I didn't feel right personally taking myself away from [my family] as much, as often as I know from past experience, that a presidential campaign requires."

Al undertook another commitment; he began writing *Earth in the Balance*, a book on the environmental crisis. In the book, Al presented an impassioned argument that the environment had reached a crisis point and that something must be done about it. The book was published in 1992, and quickly became a bestseller.

▶ This pasture was once part of the vast rain forest that covers much of Brazil. Al Gore and other environmentalists warn that the rapid cutting of forests contributes to global warming because the leaves of trees absorb $CO_2$.

▲ The Kayapó people of Brazil are just one of many groups whose traditional lives are threatened by development. In the late 1980s, the Kayapó successfully blocked the construction of a dam that would have destroyed their land.

## Earth Summit

The Earth Summit brought together people from 180 countries. The summit focused on global warming and preserving the diversity of living species on Earth.

The 1992 Earth Summit produced two agreements. One called for cutting $CO_2$ emissions over the next eight years. In the other, wealthy nations agreed to give money to poorer countries to save plant and animal species in danger of dying out. The George H.W. Bush administration objected to both agreements and refused to sign them.

In June of 1992, Al traveled to Brazil to take part in the Earth Summit. Many world leaders were there, ready to approve tough goals limiting new emissions of greenhouse gases and other steps. United States President George H. W. Bush and his Republican administration did not agree with these steps. They argued that global warming had not been proven and that drastic steps to cut back on fossil fuel use would hurt the American economy. Al blasted this stance. "The Bush administration," he said, was "the single largest obstacle to progress."

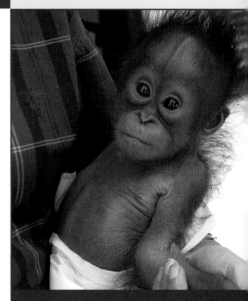

▲ An aid worker holds a baby orangutan. A type of ape, orangutans are one of the many species threatened by efforts to make economic use of natural areas.

## Chapter 5

# Vice President and Losing Candidate

I n 1992, Al Gore found himself in a new role as a national leader. He tried to push for new laws aimed at solving environmental problems, but his ability to do so would be hampered by the fact that his role was not that of president, but vice president. Eight years later, in 2000, Democrats made him their nominee for the presidency, but he suffered a bitter and controversial defeat.

## A New Team Comes To Washington

While Al was at the Earth Summit, Bill Clinton decided to choose him as his running mate for the 1992 election. Clinton, then governor of Arkansas, had defeated other candidates and became the Democratic Party nominee for president. Al had met Clinton several times and established an easy relationship with him. In addition, they agreed on most issues. Clinton appreciated the Tennessee senator's intelligence and serious approach to public policy matters. Al, like Clinton, was in his mid-40s, and would embody the message of change that Clinton promoted. He accepted Clinton's offer.

The Democrats had two rivals. President George H. W. Bush, elected in 1988, was running for re-election along with Vice President Dan Quayle of Indiana.

▲ Michigan Democrats show their enthusiastic support for the Clinton-Gore ticket during the 1992 presidential campaign. The youthful energy of the two candidates appealed to many voters.

This election also had an independent, third-party candidate, Texas billionaire H. Ross Perot. Perot's running mate was a retired admiral, James Stockdale.

On election night in November, the Clinton-Gore ticket won. They captured only 43 percent of the popular vote in the three-way race, but they won enough states to have an overwhelming victory in the electoral college—370 for Clinton-Gore compared to 168 for Bush-Quayle. (Perot-Stockdale did not win any electoral votes.)

## Vice President Gore

Clinton promised that Al would play a strong role in the Clinton administration, and he made good on that promise.

Clinton agreed that he and Al would have lunch together at least once a week so they could discuss policy issues. So much contact between a president and vice president was unusual. Clinton also gave Al Gore a leading role in issues that Al cared strongly about—nuclear arms control, the environment, and technology. The vice president also took part in most major policy meetings.

*"The global crisis is, as we say in Tennessee, real as rain, and I cannot stand the thought of leaving my children with a degraded earth and a diminished future. That's the basic reason why I have searched so intensively for ways to understand this crisis and help solve it; it is also why I am trying to convince you to be a part of the enormous change our civilization must now undergo."*

- Taken from Al Gore's 1992 bestselling book, *Earth in the Balance.*

◄ The winners celebrate their victory on election night in 1992. The four figures (from left) are Al Gore, Tipper Gore, Hillary Rodham Clinton, and president-elect Bill Clinton.

## The Electoral College

The men who wrote the United States Constitution in 1787 worried about giving too much power to the people. They came up with a system for electing a president that did not rely directly on the people. When voters cast ballots for a president, they actually choose electors, and it is the electors who pick the president. A candidate needs a majority of the electors' votes—270 out of 538.

Each state has a number of electors equal to the state's total number of members in Congress. (The District of Columbia also has three.) When a presidential candidate wins the popular vote in a state, it is his or her electors who cast their electoral votes for that state. In most states, all the electoral votes go to the winner of the popular vote. Two states use a different system that can divide the electoral votes among more than one candidate.

With this system, a candidate can win the national popular vote and still lose the election. If that candidate does not win the right combination of states, he or she will not gain a majority of electoral votes. This has been the result in a few elections—including the one in 2000.

▲ A major source of greenhouse gases is the exhaust of cars and trucks. The government requires automakers to meet certain standards of fuel consumption to try to limit the amount of fuel burned and exhaust emitted. For years, auto companies resisted making those standards tougher.

Early in 1993, Al pushed Clinton to propose a BTU tax. BTUs, or British thermal units, are a measure of the amount of energy used. Al's tax wanted to tax BTUs to encourage people and businesses to cut their energy use. Cutting energy use would, in turn, help the environment. The House passed the bill creating this tax, but senators opposed to the plan stalled the bill in the Senate. Eventually, the bill was dropped. Al had not done enough groundwork to gather support for the bill.

Environmentalists were disappointed by other actions of the new administration. Al had blasted the Bush administration for not going along with the Earth Summit goals for cutting carbon emissions. Now Clinton adopted a plan that called only for voluntary action by businesses on this issue. Since cuts were voluntary, they were unlikely to happen. Clinton also decided not to require American automakers to build cars that achieved lower fuel consumption.

Just two years into Clinton and Gore's first term, Republicans won overwhelming support from voters and gained control of the House of Representatives for the first time since 1954. Part of their agenda was to cut back on environmental laws. Al pushed Clinton to make a stand against those actions. He also convinced the leaders of environmental groups to back the White House.

Clinton managed to work with the Republicans to pass some new laws and to cast the Republicans in a negative light on other matters.

In 1996, Clinton and Gore defeated Bob Dole and Jack Kemp to win a second term.

## Successes in Government

Soon after taking office, Clinton asked Gore to lead an effort to "reinvent government" by making the departments and agencies in the executive branch (the branch that includes the president and vice president) more responsive to people's needs and more flexible in their decision making.

In September 1993, Gore released a report summarizing his recommendations on this effort. The result was impressive. Gore's nearly 400 steps would cut federal spending by $108 billion and eliminate more than 250,000 unnecessary jobs. Unfortunately in the end, though, the reforms fell far short of Gore's goals.

Al Gore's interest in technology had him work on the government to make large amounts of information available to the public over the Internet for the first time. He also worked for a bill that opened the way for telephone and cable companies to provide higher speed Internet access and led efforts to connect schools to the Internet.

▲ As global temperatures rise, scientists warn that some parts of Earth will receive less rainfall than has been normal in the past. In areas where rainfall was just enough to sustain crops, and people living off them, the result can be devastating droughts, and widespread hunger and suffering.

▶ Protestors at Kyoto criticized the slow progress toward a plan to cut greenhouse gas emissions. The dinosaur represents the fact that fossil fuels developed from the remains of animals that died millions of years ago.

サヨナラ！化石燃料

GREENPEACE

DINOSAUR DIPLOMACY 1; CLIMATE 0

GREENPEACE

## Measuring Climate Change

To measure climate change, scientists look at three kinds of information. The first is average temperatures in various places around the world. The second is the level of the world's oceans, and the third is the amount of snow and ice covering cold regions.

Many scientists say that all of these measures show that temperatures have been going up in recent decades.

## Al at Kyoto

In 1996, the environment was again, a hot issue. That year, the IPCC issued its first report on global warming. That report was a warning. Earth's temperature had risen one degree Fahrenheit (0.56 degrees Celsius) in the past century, the scientists said, and it may well rise even faster in the future.

An international meeting was set for Kyoto, Japan, the following year. It was supposed to be a follow-up to the Earth Summit of 1992. The original proposals Clinton approved for Kyoto were modest, which frustrated Al. He worked to convince Clinton to agree to tougher plans and then flew to Japan to begin the process of convincing other countries to agree to them. The final agreement that resulted from this effort called for deep cuts in American greenhouse gas emissions. As Al had expected, this plan met strong objections, and Congress never approved the agreement. Al felt, though, that he had taken an important step since many nations in the world did agree to the strict standard.

Late in his second term, Clinton faced a challenge to his political survival. Clinton had stated under oath that he had not had an inappropriate relationship with a young White House aide. Republicans in Congress charged that the denial was a lie, which meant he had committed perjury. They said that the crime of perjury was grounds for impeachment. The House voted to impeach Clinton in late December of 1998. The Senate trial took place the following January and February. In the end, the Senate voted to acquit Clinton, and he remained in office. Still, the scandal left a taint on the administration.

## Election in the Balance

As the 2000 presidential election loomed, Al had years of experience in Washington and a record as vice president during an administration that saw the economy grow rapidly. Still, he faced a

### Measuring Greenhouse Gases

In order to measure the quantity of greenhouse gases, scientists drilled pipes into Arctic and Antarctic ice and removed samples. Along with the ice, they also retrieved air bubbles trapped tens of thousands of years ago. Then they simply measured the gas in that air. By taking air bubbles trapped at different points in the past, they can see how levels have changed over time.

Using these results, scientists have concluded that the amount of greenhouse gases in the air has increased greatly over the past 200 years. They have concluded that this is due to the widespread burning of fossil fuels. They base this conclusion on two sets of facts. First, some gases they found do not occur in nature but are only the product of human activity. Second, concentrations of these gases are higher north of the Equator in regions that have more people and more industry.

▲ This scientist is storing one of hundreds of samples taken from the Greenland ice shelf. The samples are stored at temperatures well below freezing to keep them intact. The samples will be examined for evidence of global warming caused by rising $CO_2$ levels.

**Bleached Coral**
Another sign of the stresses on nature caused by global warming is the bleaching of coral. A coral reef is formed from tiny animals called coral polyps. When they die, the polyps leave behind a hard limestone structure that is home to many fish, plants, and other living things. Healthy coral (top) is colorful and vibrant. High ocean temperatures damage the coral, and leave coral colorless (bottom)—the reason for the name "coral bleaching"—and less able to support other life.

challenge for winning the Democratic nomination from former senator Bill Bradley. Despite some difficulties, Al defeated Bradley in the primaries and became the Democratic nominee. He chose Connecticut Senator Joseph Lieberman as his running mate.

The Republican nominee was George W. Bush, son of the president whom Clinton had defeated back in 1992. Bush had been governor of Texas since 1995.

The campaign was long and tough. On election night, the 2000 presidential contest proved to be one of the closest presidential races in history. Based on early results, it seemed that Al would win the popular vote and enough electoral votes to win the election. As more results came in though, television networks changed their predictions about the electoral vote. Early the next morning, they said that Bush had won Florida, and had won the election. Just a few hours later, with more votes in, they withdrew that claim, too.

Nearly two weeks after the election, Florida released its official vote count. It said that Bush had won the state's popular vote by fewer than 550 votes, giving him its electoral votes. That gave Bush 271 electoral votes—one more than he needed to win.

In the intervening days, controversies

arose. Some had to do with how ballots were constructed and how votes were cast. The only way of knowing exactly who won Florida, said Al's supporters, would be to carefully recount the ballots.

## A Fateful Decision

After the Florida announcement, Al's campaign asked three counties to conduct recounts. The recount process dragged on in fits and starts with lawsuits and counter-lawsuits arguing about the process.

Eventually, a key lawsuit reached the Florida Supreme Court, the highest court in the state. Before the justices on this court could make their final ruling, however, the justices of the United States Supreme Court, the highest court in the land, took up issue. After listening to both sides and studying the legal issues, the nine justices on the Supreme Court issued their ruling. Five of the nine—a majority—ruled that the recounts should stop and the original decision stand. George W. Bush had won Florida and the presidency.

All five of the justices who voted in favor of Bush had been named to the Court by Republican presidents. Critics said that the ruling was based on party loyalty and not legal principles. After weeks of uncertainty, Al Gore believed it was time to move on. The day after the Supreme Court issued its decision, he gave a nationwide television address. He accepted the decision and brought the bitter dispute over the election to a close.

*"The U.S. Supreme Court has spoken. Let there be no doubt, while I strongly disagree with the court's decision, I accept it. I accept the finality of this outcome."*

- Al Gore speaking after accepting defeat in the 2000 election

▲ An election official closely examines ballots in Palm Beach County, Florida, during the hotly disputed 2000 presidential election. When the United States Supreme Court ruled that George W. Bush be declared the winner in Florida, Al Gore reluctantly accepted the court's decision and became one of only a few candidates ever to win the popular vote nationally but lose in the electoral college.

## Chapter 6

# Environmental Activist

**A**fter his difficult defeat in the 2000 presidential election, Al Gore needed time to regroup. Once again, doing so led him to adopt a new purpose, but it was not really a new one. Al's re-examination made him realize that he wanted to sound the alarm about the problem of global warming—the problem he had first begun thinking about as a college student back in the 1960s.

## Regrouping

In the first months after the election, Al searched for something to do. He worked as a visiting professor at Middle Tennessee State University and other schools. He taught courses on promoting stronger communities and on strengthening families.

Al also worked with Tipper on two books, both examining modern American family life and both published late in 2002.

## Speaking Out Against Climate Change

Back when Al worked on *Earth in the Balance*, he had the idea of doing the book as a package with a television series. For years, Al had collected charts, graphs, and photographs on climate change. He had assembled them into a slide show, which he used as the centerpiece of talks to groups

▲ A boat was left perched atop a car after the flooding caused in 2005 by the powerful Hurricane Katrina. Katrina forced hundreds of thousands of people to leave their homes and covered New Orleans in water. Al and others warn that global warming will lead to even more deadly storms.

◄ Al and Tipper Gore take a moment from a book-signing ceremony to hold copies of their two books on the American family. Tipper's photographs in *The Spirit of Family* show the variety and resilience of families today, and the love that family members hold for one another.

around the world about the issue. In 2005, Tipper urged him to turn that talk into a book summarizing the current state of knowledge about climate change. That suggestion became the spark for writing *An Inconvenient Truth*. Al thought that images could help clarify his ideas about the threat of global warming and give his arguments more impact.

Al published the book in 2006. *An Inconvenient Truth* collects scientific data in text and images to show that climate change is happening and that the consequences of global warming will be terrible for humankind. Graphs show rises in temperature in recent decades and the buildup of $CO_2$ and other greenhouse gases in the atmosphere. Images taken by satellites in space portray the rapid melting of glaciers in Greenland and Antarctica. Dramatic maps drawn through computer programs reveal the impact on low-lying areas such as Florida, the San Francisco Bay area, and New York City, as well as other sites around the world, if these ice caps

### Celebrating Family Life

The Gore family has its own literary tradition that started even before *An Inconvenient Truth*. In their book *Joined at the Heart*, the Gores probe the trends affecting families today, how they cope with various problems, and how family members help each other.

Their second book, *The Spirit of Family*, is a collection of photographs that portrays the diversity of American families and the joys, sorrows, and love that family members share.

▶ ▼ Polar bears use the Arctic Sea ice for hunting seals. Year by year, the ice is melting and the bears are losing their hunting grounds. These hungry bears, shown at right, look for food at a trash dump. The photos below show the extent of the sea ice in 1979, and then the reduced sea ice in 2005.

continue to melt and sea levels rise. The book also includes some of Al's personal reflections on the issue and important people and places in his life.

## Reaching a Wider Audience

Al's message would soon gain an even wider audience. Movie producers concerned about the issue of climate change had seen his slide show and wanted to turn it into a movie. Al was skeptical at first, but he agreed to join the project. The documentary version of *An Inconvenient Truth* was released in 2006, the same year that the book was published. It became very popular and spread Al's message around the world.

Critics have faulted Al's stance. They say his claims of the effects of climate change are too extreme and that he ignores contradictory evidence. They charge that he ignores the economic and social problems that will result if societies adopt the steps he suggests. Al responds to these charges at different points of the book.

## The 2008 Election

While working on the climate change issue, Al largely avoided politics. He did make speeches critical of George W. Bush's administration, not just on the climate change issue, but he did nothing to become more active in political matters. Some people wondered if he would run for president again in 2004.

He answered that question two years before the election by flatly stating he would not do so. When Massachusetts Senator John Kerry received the Democratic Party's nomination for president that year, Al campaigned for him.

When another election loomed four years later, some supporters spoke once more about launching a movement to force him to run. Al again declared that he had no interest in running for the presidency. He refused to back either Senator Barack Obama of Illinois or Senator Hillary Clinton of New York while they fought each other for the Democratic nomination. Once Obama won that contest, Al announced his support. Before Obama spoke at the Democratic national convention that year, Al gave a speech enthusiastically endorsing him.

### What Is a Carbon Footprint?

Many environmental activists—people who want to take steps to help the environment—urge people to help prevent global warming by reducing their "carbon footprint." What does that phrase mean?

A carbon footprint is, simply, a measure of how much carbon is sent into the atmosphere based on the amount of energy a person uses. It takes into account where a person lives and how many people live in the home, what kind of car the person owns and how many miles it is driven each year, monthly electric use, and the amount of heating oil, natural gas, and propane the person uses.

Note that the carbon footprint only measures the amount of $CO_2$ a person releases into the atmosphere. It does not measure the emission of methane or other greenhouse gases.

◀ Tons of trash have been dumped into this landfill. Al urges people to reuse and recycle products and to buy those with less packaging. These steps will help fight global warming by cutting the energy needed to produce packaging.

### What Can You Do?

Al calls his message an "inconvenient" truth because, he says, it means "we are going to have to change the way we live our lives."

What kinds of changes will help? Here are just a few of the recommendations Al gives.

To Cut Electricity Use:

- Use energy-efficient light bulbs, like compact fluorescent light (CFLs) such as the one shown below.
- Use energy-efficient appliances and electronic equipment.
- Raise the home's thermostat in summer to cut air-conditioning; lower it in winter to cut heating; and insulate the home to reduce the need for either.
- Use less hot water by taking short showers and washing clothes and dishes in warm, rather than hot, water.
- Unplug appliances when not in use to prevent them from continuing to use energy.

▶ Even simple steps like buying locally grown food and reusing shopping bags can help cut greenhouse gas emissions. Anything that saves energy can help!

## Continuing the Fight

While not active in politics, Al was active in environmental causes, launching several projects to advance action against global warming. In 2004 he joined with others to create a company called Generation Investment Management. This is an investment fund that suggests people invest in companies with environmentally friendly business practices.

In 2006, he founded the Alliance for Climate Protection to promote efforts to use less energy. This nonprofit organization receives all the profits that Al earns from his part in the book and movie of *An Inconvenient Truth*. It also encourages other people to contribute. The Alliance works to bring more people into the fight to prevent climate change, in part through an effort called the We Campaign. Several large non-profits and groups such as the Girl Scouts of America have joined that campaign.

That same year, Al founded The Climate Project. This group recruits and trains volunteers around the country, and around the world, to teach others about climate change.

When he talks about climate change, Al Gore communicates two important messages. The first is that global warming is a serious crisis. The other is that drastic results are not inevitable. To make this point, Al explains that in the Chinese and Japanese written languages, the character for the word *crisis* combines the characters for two other words—danger and opportunity. In Al's eyes, the need to take steps to stop global warming also give humans a chance to change the way they live for the better. It will be better not only for the environment, but also for people.

**What Can You Do?**
To Reduce Energy
in Transportation:
- Cut the number of miles (km) driven by combining trips, using mass transit, biking, or walking.
- Buy vehicles with high gas-mileage or vehicles that are hybrids.
- Buy biofuels—fuels derived from plants—rather than gasoline.
- Buy vehicles that can run on biofuels.

As a Consumer:
- Buy fewer goods and things that last rather than need to be replaced.
- Reduce waste by refusing to buy goods with high amounts of packaging and by recycling.
- Use reusable grocery bags rather than plastic bags.
- Turn food waste into compost, which can be spread in gardens to help new plants grow, rather than throw it away.

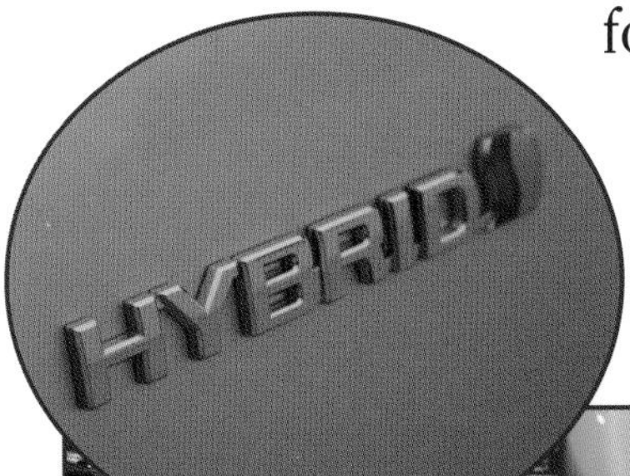

HYBRID

POWER CONTROL UNIT

ENGINE

Electricity

GENERATOR

POWE

◀ A model of a hybrid engine is shown here. The engine of a hybrid car uses gasoline sparingly, only to start and gain speed. For most of a drive, the car is powered by electricity, which does not emit greenhouse gases.

Driving less and eating less meat—two recommendations he makes—both help the environment and give people healthier lives.

Caring for the environment does more than prevent disaster. It also puts people in balance with Earth once again. To Al Gore, saving the environment also means saving humanity, not just physically, but spiritually.

▲ Activists march to push governments to act to reduce greenhouse gases. As Al explains, individuals can do much to help fight global warming simply by making energy-saving choices.

▼ Al Gore says: "We have everything we need to begin solving this crisis." If we act, we can save our collective home, planet Earth.

# Chronology

| | |
|---|---|
| **1948** | Albert Gore, Jr. is born on March 31 |
| **1965** | Meets Tipper Aitcheson at graduation dance. Graduates from St. Albans School on June 5 |
| **1969** | Graduates from Harvard on June 12. Enlists in army in August |
| **1970** | Marries Tipper on May 19 |
| **1971** | Serves in Vietnam. Discharged from army. Studies at Vanderbilt University's Divinity School. Begins work at *Nashville Tennessean* |
| **1973** | Karenna Gore born on August 6 |
| **1974** | Begins law school at Vanderbilt |
| **1976** | Wins election to the United States House of Representatives |
| **1977** | Sworn in as a member of the House on January 4 |
| **1980** | Becomes interested in issue of nuclear arms control |
| **1982** | Outlines nuclear arms control plan in the House in March |
| **1984** | Wins election to the United States Senate on November 9 |
| **1987** | Launches campaign for Democratic nomination for president |
| **1988** | Withdraws from presidential race on April 21 |
| **1989** | Albert Gore III hit by a car and seriously injured on April 3. Introduces bill to expand Internet in May |
| **1990** | Begins writing *Earth in the Balance* after being re-elected to Senate |
| **1992** | *Earth in the Balance* published in January. Attends Earth Summit. Picked as running mate by Democratic presidential candidate Bill Clinton. Clinton and Gore win the election |
| **1996** | Clinton and Gore win re-election |
| **1997** | Attends Kyoto meeting on the environment |
| **2000** | Wins popular vote but loses election for president to George W. Bush after Supreme Court decision decides Florida's electoral vote count |
| **2001** | Al teaches at several universities as a visiting professor |
| **2002** | Publishes two books, with Tipper, on the modern American family |
| **2004** | Co-founds Generation Investment Management |
| **2006** | Publishes the book *An Inconvenient Truth*. Documentary film *An Inconvenient Truth* released. Founds the Alliance for Climate Protection and The Climate Project |
| **2007** | Co-winner, with Intergovernmental Panel on Climate Change (IPCC), of Nobel Peace Prize on October 12 |
| **2008** | With others, accepts Academy Award for *An Inconvenient Truth* |

# Glossary

**acquit**  To find a person accused of a crime not guilty after a trial

**administration**  A collective term for all the officials working in the executive branch of the United States government under the direction of the president

**atmosphere**  The layer of air above Earth, made mainly of nitrogen, oxygen, and other gases, which allows plants and animals to live

**bill**  A proposal for a new law; to become a law, a bill must be passed by both houses of Congress and signed by the president (or, if vetoed by the president, passed again by a two-thirds majority in each house)

**casualties**  In war, the number of members of the armed forces who are killed, wounded, taken prisoner, or missing as a result of combat

**civil rights**  The rights that each citizen enjoys as a result of being a citizen, such as the right to equal opportunity and to vote

**communist**  A person who believes in Communism. Communism is a political philosophy based on an economic system where a country's natural resources, businesses, and industry are owned by all the people and controlled by the government

**constituent**  A person whom a member of Congress represents

**convention**  A meeting at which political party members choose their nominees for office

**documentary**  A movie about actual people and events, rather than fictional stories

**draft**  A system that requires people to serve in the armed forces. The draft ended in the United States in 1973 when the all-volunteer army was adopted

**drought**  A long period of time with little or no rain, which can lead to crop failure and widespread hunger

**equator**  The imaginary line around the middle of Earth, which divides the world into the Northern and Southern Hemispheres

**federal government**  The national government of the United States that includes Congress, the president and the executive branch departments and agencies, and the United States Supreme Court and lower courts

**fossil fuels**  Fuels such as oil, gasoline, natural gas, and coal, which are burned to produce energy

**global warming**  The increase in overall average temperatures on Earth in recent decades mainly because of the increased burning of fossil fuels

**greenhouse gases**  Chemicals such as $CO_2$, methane, and others released into the air when fossil fuels are burned and that build up in the atmosphere, causing global warming

**hearings** Official sessions in the United States Congress in which members of Congress question witnesses, including experts and ordinary people, about problems facing the country

**impeachment** The process of formally charging a public official with committing a crime and trying him or her to determine guilt. In the case of the impeachment of the president of the United States, in the first step a majority of the House of Representatives must vote to charge that the president committed a crime or crimes. In the second step, the Senate holds a trial, with each senator voting on the president's guilt or innocence. If two-thirds of the senators find the president guilty, he or she can be removed from office. If fewer than two-thirds find the president guilty, he or she is acquitted and remains in office

**investigative reporting** A kind of reporting that involves digging out facts and may lead to developing stories involving political corruption or illegal or unethical actions by people in power

**investment fund** A business that recommends ways for people to invest their money

**leftist** Someone who favors a strong governmental role in solving social and economic issues. Liberals, socialists, and communists may be considered leftists in differing degrees

**major** The subject in which a college student concentrates, taking more courses in this field than any others

**moderate** Political positions that are neither very conservative nor very liberal

**national security** Issues related to defense, the armed forces, and weapons systems

**nominee** A person officially chosen by a political party to run for a political office

**nonprofit organization** A group that does work but, unlike a business, does not aim to earn a profit

**parts per million** How scientists state the concentration of one substance in a gas, liquid, or solid. The higher the number of parts per million, the more of the substance, such as a greenhouse gas, is found in the gas, liquid, or solid, such as the atmosphere

**popular vote** The total number of votes a candidate receives in an election

**primary** An election in which voters who belong to a particular party choose their candidate to run in the general election, when all voters choose which person will actually hold an office

**radical** A person who favors extreme solutions to political issues

## Books

Bily, Cynthia A. (ed.) *Global Warming* (Opposing Viewpoints).
Greenhaven Press, 2006.

Gore, Al. *Earth in the Balance: Ecology and the Human Spirit*. Rodale, 2006.

Gore, Al. *An Inconvenient Truth: The Planetary Emergency of Global Warming
and What We Can Do About It*. Rodale, 2006.

Knauer, Kelly. *Global Warming* (Time). Twenty-First Century Books, 2007.

Landau, Elaine. *The 2000 Presidential Election* (Cornerstones of Freedom).
Children's Press, 2002.

Robinson, Matthew. *America Debates Global Warming: Crisis or Myth?*
(America Debates). Rosen, 2008.

## Web sites

*blog.algore.com*
At this site, Al Gore posts comments on environmental and other public issues.

*globalwarmingkids.net/*
Created by ClimateChangeEducation.org, this site has information, activities, and
other features aimed at children.

*www.epa.gov/climatechange/kids/*
The U.S. Environmental Protection Agency's children's site on the issue of climate
change includes background information and actions that individuals can take.

*www.pewclimate.org/global-warming-basics/kidspage.cfm*
This portion of the Web site of the Pew Center on Global Climate Change addresses
children with basic discussions of global warming and links to other sites.

*www.unep.org/Tunza/*
The Web site of the United Nations Environment Programme has sections for
children, each with more information on global warming and other issues.

*www.wecansolveit.org/*
Official Web site of the Alliance for Climate Protection, a group founded by Al Gore
and others to provide education about global warming and action to combat it.

# Index

**About the Author**
Dale Anderson lives in eastern Pennsylvania, where he has written dozens of books on history and other subjects. He enjoys cooking, birdwatching, movies, puzzles, and sports.

Printed in the U.S.A. — CG